Tiger's birthday
and
Cat and Dove

Hannie Truijens

Nelson

Cat and Dove

Cat saw Dove up in the tree.
Dove looked fat and good to eat.
"I will play a trick on Dove,"
said Cat.

"Come down, Dove," said Cat.
"Lion said that we must all
be friends.
So I won't eat you."

3

Dove looked down at Cat.
Cat looked big and strong.
"This is a trick," said Dove.
"You will eat me if I come down."

"No," said Cat.

"It isn't a trick.

We are all friends now.

Fox and Hen are friends.

Owl and Rat are also friends."

Dove looked back.

"Here comes Dog," she said.

"You must not run away.

You and Dog are friends now."

"Oh no," said Cat.
"Dog wasn't there so he didn't
hear what Lion said.
Goodbye, Dove."

7

But there wasn't any dog.
Dove came down from the tree
to eat.
"I can play tricks too,"
she said.

Tiger's birthday

"It is Tiger's birthday,"
said Helen.
"Can she have a party, Mum?"
"Yes," said Mum.

Helen went to look for Sulima
and Liz and Beth.
She went to look for Jack and
Colin and Ali.
"Come to a party," she said.

"It is Tiger's birthday,"
said Helen.
"Cats don't have birthdays,"
said Liz.
"Well, Tiger does," said Helen.

"This is Tiger's present,"
said Helen.
"Cats don't get presents,"
said Beth.
"Well, Tiger does," said Helen.

"This is Tiger's birthday cake,"
said Helen.
"Cats don't have birthday cakes,"
said Sulima.
"Well, Tiger does," said Helen.

"You must all sing
happy birthday to Tiger,"
said Helen.

"I said you must all sing
happy birthday to Tiger,"
said Helen.

"I will have a birthday party
for my dog," said Colin.
"You can all come."